The 17th-century
Dolls'houses
of the Rijksmuseum

Jet Pijzel - Dommisse

RIJKS MUSEUM
amsterdam

Maids and peasants
from the dolls' house of
Petronella Dunois,
right to left: 'Clear
Starcher', Wet nurse,
Kitchenmaid, Waterland
peasant, Peasantboy
Teunis

Contents

Seventeenth-century dolls' houses

In the second half of the 17th century dolls' houses were made in Amsterdam for a small group of well-to-do women of the regent and merchant classes. There now survive three of which the outer cabinet, the rooms and their furnishings still constitute a unified whole. Two of these can be seen in the Rijksmuseum, the third, that of Petronella de la Court, is on display in the Central Museum in Utrecht. These dolls' houses, ingeniously made for show, were filled with extremely fragile objects of, for example, porcelain, ivory or glass. Thus they were not meant for children, but for grown-up women.

The dolls' houses fit into the tradition of 'collectors' cabinets', richly decorated cupboards in which collections of art objects were kept, but in their case the contents consisted of miniature objects which together portrayed a complete domestic inventory. In Holland the cupboard took the form not of a house, but of a cabinet. The unique contents were kept behind closed doors and still further protected by a curtain, as can be seen from a painting of Petronella Oortman's dolls' house.

The dolls' house and its contents represented the combined efforts of many skilled craftsmen: painters, cabinet-makers, sculptors, silversmiths, basket-makers and glassblowers. Their work was probably coordinated by the women who commissioned it, although a sort of architect may have been involved in the furnishing of the large dolls' house of Petronella Oortman.

Dolls' houses now provide valuable information about the furnishing of houses in the late 17th century. They contain objects of which scarcely any full-scale examples have survived and they show us how not only fine ladies and gentlemen, but also a kitchen-maid and a laundry-maid were dressed.

a Jacob Appel, The
dolls' house of
Petronella Oortman,
c. 1710
Oil on parchment
87 x 69 cm
b The dolls' house of
Petronella Dunois,
closed
c The dolls' house of
Petronella de la Court,
1670-1690
Collection: Central Museum,
Utrecht

a

b

c

The dolls' house of Petronella Oortman

The dolls' house of Petronella Oortman (1656-1716) has always been regarded as a sort of wonder of the world. It was long thought to have been commissioned by Tsar Peter the Great, who was supposed to have rejected it as too expensive.

The cabinet is a work of art in itself, being decorated all over with marquetry of tortoiseshell and finely engraved pewter. These materials were only rarely used in Holland and the maker had apparently worked at the French court before moving to Amsterdam. On the sides of the cabinet appears a cipher of the initials B and O of Johannes Brandt (1654-1731) and his wife Petronella Oortman. This occurs again at various other places in the dolls' house, such as on the carving above the hall, on the coverlet of the lying-in bed and on napkins.

The wealthy widow Petronella Oortman married the silk merchant Johannes Brandt in 1686. They lived in Warmoesstraat in Amsterdam. The cabinet of the dolls' house was probably made between 1686 and 1690, while the furnishing, which is remarkably true to life in both proportions and materials, took another fifteen years to complete. A reliable source informs us that Petronella Oortman spent 20,000-30,000 guilders on her dolls' house.

In the painting of it, which the artist Jacob Appel must have made shortly after its completion, the contents are acccurately portrayed, while they are described in detail in a printed catalogue of the second half of the 18th century. Scarcely any objects were added at a later date, but two of the areas were altered somewhat in the course of the 18th century: the garden behind the hall has disappeared and what is now the tapestry room was originally shrouded in mourning. Of the dolls only a baby has survived.

The German traveller Zacharias von Uffenbach wrote an intriguing description of a visit to the dolls' house in 1718, emphasizing its function as a showcase full of surprises, which could fascinate one for many hours.

a The dolls' house of Petronella Oortman, Amsterdam, 1686-1705
Cabinet, oak, veneered with tortoiseshell and pewter
Height 255 cm, length 190 cm, width 78 cm

b Coverlet of lying-in bed with monogram BO
c Baby from the lying-in room

b

a

c

The Linen Room

Under the sloping roofs of the tall Amsterdam houses there were various attic rooms. One of them used to be reserved for dealing with the linen which was generally sent out of the house for washing and bleaching. The damp sheets, tablecloths and shirts were dried on rods laid loosely over a rack hung from the ceiling. In this linen room there hang some napkins from the rich store in the linen cupboard of the lying-in room. They bear the initials B and O and were specially woven to size for the dolls' house.

The ironing table is covered with a soft woollen undercloth, on which the laundry-maid, now missing alas, could smooth the linen. Her two irons are of the type that was filled with glowing charcoal. They are rendered in minute detail in the normal material, brass, with iron soleplates and wooden handles. This is what makes Petronella Oortman's dolls' house so special. In other 17th-century dolls' houses they are made of silver.

Freshly-ironed washing lies in a clothes tray, while the sheets and table linen remain a bit longer in a heavy linen press. The washing is stored or carried round the house in linen baskets, with or without lids. On the wall on the right hangs a swaddling seat, a large oval basket with a high back, in which the dry-nurse or wet-nurse sat on the floor by the fire with her legs stretched out, so that she could feed the baby and then wipe its bottom on her lap in the days before a chest of drawers was used for the purpose. Normally, of course, this seat was used in the lying-in room.

Behind the linen room there are two bedrooms for the servants, each with a box-bed curtained with a floral print and with a chair and a chamberpot beside it.

a Box-beds for the maids
b Irons
Brass, iron and wood
Height 3 and 3.7 cm

b

The Peat and Provisions Loft

This storeroom is split up into different areas by a floor and a dividing wall. A ladder leads to the peat loft, where blocks of peat and bundles of split wood are neatly stacked behind the bars. Two baskets serve for carrying these important fuels from the attic to the various fireplaces in the house.

Under the peat loft is a provisions store. The panels of the dividing wall have fine fretwork scrolls similar to the scroll decoration on the outside of the dolls' house. On the shelves under the oval window there remain only a few storage jars and a rat trap.

Otherwise this attic serves as a store for various objects not needed in the house for the moment, such as an extra table or mirror. On the whitewashed wall hangs a flat basket, the bottom of which is decorated with embroidery. Beside the ladder stands an extra brazier used in the nursery and lying-in room for keeping a bowl of pap warm and drying or airing wet napkins and clothes. For this purpose a tin pan containing glowing coals was placed in the bottom of the brazier and the damp things were laid over the cover.

In summertime the numerous foot-warmers to be found in every Dutch house were neatly stowed away in the loft. Those here still contain their coal pans. The spinning wheel will also regularly have stood in the loft in many 17th-century households. With its finely-turned ebony struts it offered the turner a prime opportunity for displaying his craftsmanship in miniature.

a Stacks of wood and peat
b Spinning wheel with thread-winder
Boxwood and maple
Height 13.5 cm

a

b

The Nursery

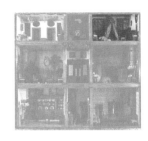

Few of the objects in this richly-appointed room suggest that it is meant as a nursery. Only a cradle with its cover affords a clue to this. In Jacob Appel's painting of the dolls' house two children are shown in this room, one of them seated on the lap of a peasant in Waterland costume. Was he a man-servant or the husband of the nursemaid?

From the beautifully painted ceiling a canopy is suspended over a child's oak bed. Although this round, tentlike structure is made of yellow silk trimmed with a pale blue gathered band, this type of bed is less imposing than a four-poster with a large tester supported by four posts at the corners. The same yellow silk, trimmed with braid, is used for the cradle and table covers and the cushions. In the late 17th century it was considered important that the upholstery, certainly in grand rooms, should match throughout.

The furnishings of the nursery are quite luxurious. Above the table on the left hangs a large mirror in a gilt bronze frame, while two oval paintings of peasant scenes in matching frames are set high up over the doors. When the shutters of the lower windows at the back are closed, they reveal on the inside colourful paintings of bouquets of flowers on a gilt ground. The upper windows contain what were then called sashes, consisting of a wooden framework covered with silk, here painted with parrots. No full-scale sashes like this have survived.

The walnut cupboard on a high stand held the children's clothes, but all that now remain are a pair of trousers, a nightshirt and two pairs of stockings.

a Cupboard for children's clothes
Oak and walnut
Height 25.3 cm

b Shirt, trousers and two pairs of stockings
Linen, wool and silk
Length (shirt) 8 cm

a

b

The Salon

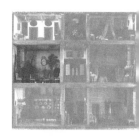

In the second half of the 17th century the salon ('zaal') was the grandest room in the house. It was not used every day, but only for the reception of guests. Its decoration and furnishings unmistakably demonstrated the wealth and status of the owner of the house.

The salon in the dolls' house is decorated with costly floor-to-ceiling wall paintings by Nicolaes Piemont featuring a continuous landscape with a cloudy sky and birds. It is as if one were standing in the middle of this decidedly non-Dutch mountainous scene, but the illusion is immediately shattered by the ponderous chimneypiece, the mirror, the folding table in the corner and the row of chairs against the wall.

The chimneypiece contains a painting by Willem van Royen of poultry in a park-like setting. The fireplace is decorated in the summer months by a large painting of a vase of flowers. Similar flowers and a parrot adorn the finely-painted top of a tea table. The black background, reminiscent of Oriental lacquer, and the black and gold decoration on the stand reflect the exotic character of tea drinking, which was still highly unusual then.

In keeping with the purpose of the salon, the chairs are the richest of all those in the dolls' house, being decorated with carving and upholstered with expensive silk velvet trimmed with braid and fringe.

The salon was used for evening entertainments at which music was made, games were played and refreshments served. In the painting by Appel two dolls sit playing backgammon and smoking pipes at a simple table consisting of a top on a separate folding stand. When the visitors had gone, it would be stowed away again and the other furniture would be neatly ranged round the walls.

a Flowerpiece attributed to Willem van Rooyen
Oil on canvas
51.5 x 68.5 cm

b Armchair
Walnut with silk velvet
Height 13.5 cm

b

The Hall

In the 17th century the hall was still spacious, with arches leading to a narrow corridor and staircase behind it. Such an arrangement is suggested in the dolls' house, despite the absence of a staircase. Since the hall was the first room the visitor entered in a rich merchant's house, it was appointed with costly materials like the white Italian marble with bands of darker ashlar on the floor here.

In the white stucco walls paintings in tones of grey are set in such a way as to suggest niches with marble sculptures and reliefs. Such grisailles with allegorical subjects and personifications were considered eminently suitable for a hall by the famous late 17th-century painter Gerard de Lairesse. Those here were probably painted by Cornelis Hoogsaat, one of his pupils. Mounted in the ceiling is a polychrome painting of Dawn seated on a cloud. This is attributed to Johannes Voorhout, who also supplied paintings for the lying-in and tapestry rooms.

In the lower area behind the arches there are also grisailles on the two doors, while Mercury, the god of commerce, hovers on the ceiling. He clearly relates to the office above this area, the 'comptoir', where the master of the house conducted his business.

The hall is furnished with two gueridons and two finely carved benches. In Appel's painting a formal garden can clearly be seen behind the arches. This was constructed in a separate box that could be inserted behind the hall. Von Uffenbach's description of 1718 mentions the remarkable fact that it included a fountain which spouted real water.

a Carving above the hall with the monogram BO
b Hall bench
Olive wood
Height 9.7 cm
c Ceiling painting, Dawn, attributed to Johannes Voorhout
Oil on panel
35 x 24.3 cm

a

b

c

The Lying-in Room

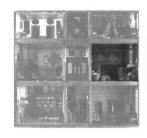

For the birth of a child a room in the house was designated as a lying-in room and specially appointed for the event. Once the baby had safely arrived and the dry-nurse hired for the purpose had neatly swaddled it and smartened up the mother, visitors could be received there. Dolls' houses are an important source of information about the arrangement of such a room.

In a deep niche or alcove at the back of the room stands the lying-in bed, a completely upholstered four-poster with a beautifully embroidered coverlet, a top sheet of fine, transparent linen and a mattress, bolster and pillow with lace-trimmed covers. The red watered silk of the bed curtains is trimmed with braids and tassels of red and yellow silk. The same material and trimming are used for the curtain of the alcove, the cradle cover, the table cover (underneath the white muslin cloth) and the cushions on the chairs. All this forms a unified whole with the red velvet on the walls.

In addition to a cradle, lying-in rooms usually contained a brazier with its cover, an invalid chair and a folding screen covered with woollen check to protect the mother and her child from draughts. The back, seat and arms of the invalid chair are completely covered with softly-padded cushions. On them, a little bit forlorn now, lies the beautifully swaddled baby, which is probably the only surviving doll from this house.

On the chest of drawers covered by two cloths stands a tea set flanked by a silver tea kettle and coffee urn made by the Amsterdam silversmith Christiaan Warenberg. The mirror with its tortoiseshell frame and the four silver wall sconces representing the four seasons contribute to the splendour of this grand room.

The choice of biblical subjects for the paintings, both signed by Johannes Voorhout, is highly appropriate for a lying-in room: the chimneypiece painting shows Pharaoh's daughter finding Moses in the wicker basket, the ceiling painting Moses with the tables of the law.

a Lying-in bed without curtains
Walnut and silk
Height 27.5 cm

b Tea kettle and stand and coffee urn by Christiaan Warenberg
Silver
Height (urn) 4.7 cm

b

In this dolls' house a distinction is made between the 'best kitchen' and the 'cookroom'. The room where the cooking was done on a cosy open fire was traditionally the family's main living room. In small houses people ate, slept and spent the greater part of the day there. During the course of the 17th century the need arose in larger houses for a separate kitchen for the cooking and a rather better furnished room for eating and displaying the fine kitchenware, although the latter was still called the 'kitchen'.

In this best kitchen there were originally three dolls, two children in the care of a nursemaid, who was busy sewing and mending. Her sewing pillow, lace pillow, sewing box and scissors still lie on the folding table, while her sewing basket stands on the floor. The smaller child sat playing on a close-stool, which has a chamber pot under the hole in the seat.

The ceiling of the kitchen is decorated with a perspective painting of a dome with glass windows. The walls are tiled from floor to ceiling. These tiles are of the normal size, but they have been painted to suggest small tiles and must have been specially made for this dolls' house kitchen. The fireplace has an additional decoration of wreathed pilasters flanking a centre panel with floral motifs, each over four tiles. On the hearth stands a chased silver fireback and a porcelain extinguisher.

The entire back wall is occupied by a large porcelain cabinet with glass doors. In 17th-century Holland porcelain was eagerly collected and put on show. The miniature porcelain here is known to have been ordered for the dolls' house in China and Japan. Behind the beautifully-painted lower doors glassware is stored. A parrot's cage, the sashes painted in the Chinese manner and the diamond-shaped black lacquer trays over the doors underline the exotic character of this splendid room.

a Parrot's cage
Tinned iron, brass and ebony
Height 11.4 cm

b Sewing pillow
Silk, metal thread and mirror glass
Length 5 cm

c Japanese dishes
Porcelain
Diameter 3.5 cm

a

c

The Cookroom

This kitchen, entirely devoted to the preparation of food, is a simple room with wooden beams, whitewashed walls and cupboards painted moss green. No cooking is going on at present, so instead of a fire on the hearth there is a brass extinguisher, in which any peat still smouldering was put out. A jack, a basket of fresh peat and a pair of bellows await further activity.

On the draining board under the window giving on to the Best Kitchen dishes of fruit and preserves stand ready. The pump with its brass handles and taps used to be able to pump real water out of a tank under the sink. Above it items of kitchen equipment hang from a black board. Behind a door at the very back of the cookroom there is a privy with a plank with a hole in it covered by a lid.

The cookroom houses a number of ordinary utensils of which scarcely any actual examples have survived from the 17th century, such as brass market buckets, a set of indoor brooms, a spoon rack and some baskets with handles, one of which is filled with minute knives and silver forks. The various candlesticks and snuffers show how well proportioned the objects in this dolls' house are in relation to each other. They are made in their original materials instead of in silver, as is the case in other 17th-century dolls' houses.

On the right wall five tankards, two of which still have gold lids, hang from cup-hooks under a board. They look as if they are made of Chinese blue and white porcelain, but are in fact of glass. A bird cage for a canary or a goldfinch was a common object in a kitchen. Over the door to the Best Kitchen hangs a highly unusual dish of red lacquer, which may have been meant as a foretaste of the Oriental treasures to be found there.

a Sconces, candlestick and snuffer
Brass and iron
Height (candlestick) 3.3 cm

b Dishes with wax fruit

a

b

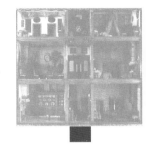

In addition to the pump spouting real water the cookroom offers more surprises. Behind the end of the draining board there is a trap-door over steps leading to a cellar below, which is built into the middle drawer of the stand of the cabinet. To get a good view of this cellar, half the floor of the cookroom must be pulled forward, but it can also be seen through a round peephole if the drawer is removed.

Even in this humble area great care has been devoted to rendering reality as closely as possible in miniature. The floor is painted to resemble brown and green flagstones and the walls are whitewashed. The shelves and the duckboards on the floor also seem to have been distempered white originally. Duckboards were essential on the damp cellar floors of Amsterdam canal houses for keeping the tubs of butter and other commodities dry.

The stocks of beer and wine were stored behind a white grille, hence the door with its fine fittings could be locked. The beer barrels, two of which still have taps, lie on a staging. On the shelf bottles stand waiting to be filled with drink. Some of them still have old corks, which are specially mentioned in the 18th-century description. The holes in the shelf were probably for storing empty bottles upside down.

The objects of green, yellow and white glass imitate cooking pots, coal pans, jars and jugs that would actually have been made of earthenware.

Buckets and tubs stand ready for heavy cleaning jobs along with a long-handled scrubbing brush, two brooms and a scrubber made of bundles of faggots. One broom seems to have got worn down already.

a Beer barrels on staging
Various woods and brass
Diameter (barrel) 4.5 cm

b Tankards, cooking pots and coal pans
Glass
Height (tankard) 3.5 cm

c Indoor and street brooms
Various woods and hog hair
Length 18 cm

a

c

The Tapestry Room

This room derives its name from the embroidered hangings with which the walls are covered. The zigzag pattern, embroidered in what was then known as Irish stitch in silk in gradated shades of green, yellow and pink, was used throughout the 17th century, but nowhere have such hangings survived in their original setting.

The ceiling and chimneypiece are beautifully painted with symmetrical acanthus scrolls and rosettes. The painting by the artist Johannes Voorhout set into the chimney breast shows Christ letting the little children come to him, a subject undoubtedly in keeping with the original purpose of the room, where a dead child was laid out in the centre, as can be seen from the painting of the dolls' house.

Against the back wall stands a highly unusual collector's cabinet filled with a collection of tiny shells, some of which are still piled up and arranged in the original decorative manner. The cabinet is decorated on the outside to imitate Oriental lacquer and on top of it stands the customary set of porcelain vases and bottles. A day-bed, the finely upholstered chairs and table and the carpet on the floor give the tapestry room a grand air.

A door in the wall hangings leads to a library behind the tapestry room. Here stands a curtained bookcase with 84 little books in colourful parchment and leather bindings. Most of them contain cut out prints of townscapes, coats of arms, maps and portraits. On a lectern stands a Bible of 1750 finely bound in gold and velvet. This is probably the only later addition to the contents of the dolls' house.

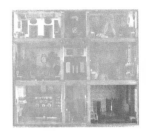

a Collector's cabinet with collection of shells
Wood lacquered black and red with gold
Height 28 cm

b Library with bookcase and reading desk

c Atlas with maps of Eastern Europe and Africa
Height 5.3 cm

a

The dolls' house of Petronella Dunois

The earliest dolls' house in the Rijksmuseum's collection is precisely dated. A pincushion in the lying-in room bears the date 1676 and the initials PD for the then 26-year-old Petronella Dunois (1650-95). Petronella was the daughter of a high official at the Stadholder's court in The Hague. After the death of her parents she came to live with her sister Maria in Amsterdam, neither of them being without means. Maria also compiled a dolls' house in Amsterdam, but this is no longer known.

When Petronella married the Leiden regent Pieter van Groenendijck in 1677, the dolls' house was accorded special mention in a list of her contributions to their household, along with a vast quantity of linen. The Rijksmuseum has recently acquired two portraits of Petronella and Pieter painted by Nicolaes Maes.

The dolls' house was handed down within the family in the female line until 1934, when it was given to the museum. It was long thought originally to have been made for Margaretha de Ruyter, who is known to have possessed a dolls' house in a similar cabinet.

The dolls' house of Petronella Dunois is built into a cabinet veneered with walnut marquetry in a geometrical pattern of rosettes and stars. Originally it could be closed off by two doors in which right from the beginning there were two glass windows at the level of the most important rooms, the 'Lying-in Room' and the 'Best Room'.

There still exists an inventory of the dolls' house, which may have been made between 1730 and 1740 and was later transcribed. From this it is clear that most of the original 17th-century contents, including twenty splendid dolls, have survived. Continual small additions in the shape of both old 17th-century objects and new ones were made to the dolls' house in later years, so that there is now much more in it than was originally the case.

a Dolls' house of Petronella Dunois, Amsterdam, c. 1676 with later additions
Cabinet, oak, veneered with walnut
Height 200 cm, length 149 cm, width 56 cm

b Pincushion with initials and date 1676
Silk and silver thread
3.5 x 4 cm

c Nicolaes Maes, portraits of Petronella Dunois and Pieter van Groenendijck, c. 1680
Oil on canvas
69.5 x 57.8 cm

b

a

c

The Peat Loft

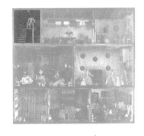

Not much can be done with a peat loft as regards decoration, yet this area played such an important role in houses that it is to be found in all the surviving 17th-century dolls' houses. Here, after all, was kept the stock of peat, which had increasingly replaced wood as a fuel in the second half of the 17th century. Without peat it would have been impossible to survive the cold, wet winters.

Peat was delivered to the houses in large, often numbered baskets, while indoors the servants carried the blocks of peat to their destinations in smaller baskets. The inventory of the dolls' house lists one basket with a handle and one without. Both have survived and are crammed full of miniature blocks of real peat. These 17th-century baskets are woven of finely split osier with darker stripes.

The funny fellow leaning over the balustrade of the upper loft is probably to be counted among the servants of the household. He has a hump and is pulling a face. On his head he wears a pointed hat and under his coarse linen coat striped baggy trousers and stockings to match. This 17th-century doll seems to have strayed out of a travelling show and precisely what he is doing in the peat loft of a fine house is not entirely clear.

Under the upper loft there is a cubby-hole painted red and yellow and containing a close-stool which, like some of the 17th-century furniture in the nursery, is made of nicely-painted cardboard.

a Servant

Height 15 cm

b Peat baskets

Osier and peat

Height (with handle) 9 cm

a

b

The Linen Room

A trellis separates the peat loft from the linen room, which is immediately recognizable from the rack with the drying rods. The doll behind the table is called the 'clear-starcher' in the old inventory. She is ironing the starched linen with a large silver iron on two 'folding' or ironing tables consisting of separate table-tops on trestles. There are three smaller folding tables for her use as well. Table-tops and trestles that were easy to store are mentioned in many 17th- and 18th- century household inventories. They were used as dining or card tables as well as working surfaces.

Petronella Dunois was not overly concerned about correct proportions in her dolls' house, as can be seen from the silver linen-press. This miniature may have been in her possession for some time before she had the dolls' house made, for silver linen-presses are often found in collections of silver toys.

The tall basket chair with wings is an invalid chair. The covered basket and linen basket are full of linen and clothes. This dolls' house contains interesting garments such as shirts, caps and covers for swaddling clothes, all richly trimmed with lace. On a stand in the corner lie blankets of brushed white wool edged with pale blue silk ribbon. No ordinary full-size woollen blankets have survived from the 17th century.

This attic also contains cleaning implements: brushes, brooms and a mop with finely turned handles. A great variety of brooms and brushes like this are to be found in all the old dolls' houses, but it is not always clear nowadays precisely what they were each used for.

a Basket with linen and clothes
Osier, linen
Height (closed) 8 cm

b Children's clothes
Linen
Length (shirt) 8.7 cm

b

The Nursery

The most spectacular object in this nursery is the bed with silk curtains and four finials of tufts of silk and real feathers. This is the only dolls' house in which the two four-posters still have their original finials, such as must have graced many a grand bed in the 17th century. The bed itself is actually quite simply made of painted wood, cardboard and paper. The mattress is covered by a padded quilt of flowered chintz lined with silk and a child's jacket of the same material lies in the sewing basket.

A seemstress is keeping an eye on the children. The clothes of this 17th-century doll were supplemented in the 18th century by one of the popular chintz jackets of the day and a large white cap, under which her 17th-century cap and gold hairpin are well preserved. A sewing basket, a spinning wheel, a yardstick and a pair of scissors, the last three made of silver, belong among her equipment.

The nursery houses three little children, one on a painted cardboard close-stool, one in a cradle and one in a walking-frame. The last two were added in the 18th century. So too were the three 'rush-bottomed' chairs made of plaited spills of rolled paper. Their pale blue silk cushions match the colours of the bed.

Over the door hangs a charming drawing of a snow scene. In the hearth stands an appropriate object for a nursery, a fireguard, here made of silver, which was placed round the fire to keep the children at a distance.

a Seamstress
Height approx. 18 cm

b Child in walking-frame
Height 9 cm

c Quilt
Cotton and silk
12 x 17 cm

b

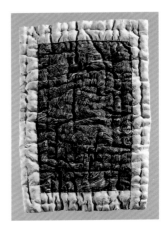

c

The Lying-in Room

The lying-in room of Petronella Dunois, who was herself childless, is the earliest surviving interior in which the walls and bed are hung with chintz. This brightly-painted washable flowered cotton was shipped to Holland from India in increasing quantities in the 17th century, but only a few coverlets and quilts survive from that period. Hence this room is an important illustration of the use of chintz for interior decoration around 1675. Chintz remained highly popular right through the 18th century.

The chintz of the four-poster with its imposing finials is trimmed with galloon, fringe and tassels in matching colours. The new mother is still lying comfortably in bed between fine linen sheets and against three pillows richly trimmed with lace. She is being looked after by a rather boorish looking nurse, known as 'the crosspatch', and a dry-nurse in Waterland costume, who is feeding the babies. The father has come to admire his offspring, evidently a pair of twins since the inventory mentions a son and a daughter. The little boy is still lying naked in the cradle, while his sister, already tightly swaddled, is lying on a christening-cloth on the wet-nurse's lap.

In the oldest photograph of this dolls' house the pincushion with the date and the initials PD appears in this room. It further contains a large number of miniature silver objects of the 17th century, such the firebacks, two pokers, tongues, shovel and brush, two wall sconces, a ewer and basin and two large candlesticks. The room also has a fine set of baskets, including a baby basket, a brazier and a swaddling seat. The exceptionally interesting folding screen, which is described in the earliest inventory as 'lacquered', must already have been brought from Japan in the late 17th century. The decoration and the technique of stencilled motifs and gold leaf in relief on paper is unmistakably Japanese.

a Cradle with padded quilt

Osier, silk, linen, the baby of wax

Height (cradle) 9 cm

b Japanese folding screen

Wood, paper and copper

Height 18.4 cm

a

b

The old name 'Best Room' immediately characterizes this salon as a reception room adorned with the most fashionable and expensive furniture and works of art. Just as in the lying-in room, the ceiling is painted, the walls are hung with fabric - yellow silk in this case - and the floor is veneered with various types of wood in a geometric pattern with stars which echoes the plan of the ceiling. No parquet floors like this have survived in 17th-century Dutch houses and it is questionable whether there actually were any at that time. It is quite possible that the floors of the finest rooms in the dolls' house were given additional decoration regardless of whether this reflected reality.

The cabinet and the tops of the three tables are also decorated with marquetry with stars and rosettes in olive wood. The cabinet contains valuables and linen, an important possession of 17th-century housewives. The table-cloths and napkins and the as yet unmade-up bolts of linen lie neatly on cupboard cloths edged with lace. The pieces of porcelain that were set on the cabinet in the mid-18th century are highly unusual: a seven-piece garniture of Meissen porcelain minutely painted with flowers.

The four 'tabourets', the wall rack with ivory uprights and the ten round ebony reliefs belong to the 17th-century inventory. Eight of the reliefs show heads of famous emperors, possibly sawn out of boxwood draughtsmen made earlier in Southern Germany. The colourful miniatures painted on ivory are 19th-century additions.

There are three children and two ladies in the best room. Are they waiting to visit the lying-in room? At all events, the hair of the two women is beautifully dressed and they are wearing dresses with trains richly trimmed with gold and silver lace.

a 'Tabouret'
Walnut, silk with silver thread
Height 5.5 cm

b Two visitors
Height 20 cm

c Cabinet, filled with linen and valuables; on top a Meissen cupboard garniture
Olive wood on oak, linen, glass, gold, porcelain
Height (cabinet) 20.3 cm

a

b

c

The cellar in this dolls' house is richly stocked with foodstuffs. On the shelves stand dishes with pies, chickens and a cow's head. The bottles of oil and the glass storage jars with herbs are sealed with leather covers or a cloth soaked in oil. Little walnuts lie in a basket, dried fish hang on the wall. Five small barrels of turned maple are filled to the brim with 'butter', which is decorated on top with an incised pattern. These and the fish undoubtedly belong to the 17th-century inventory.

Other fine examples of 17th-century turning are the various tubs, barrels, casks and other containers. Salted meat was among the items stored in the barrels with lids. Behind the open partition an imposing row of barrels with silver taps lies on a staging. The inventory differentiates between wine and beer barrels. Painted on the front of the three beer barrels are a white cloverleaf, a swan and a horn respectively. These probably indicate the names of real breweries. For example, the 'Swan' brewery on the Singel, the canal where Petronella Dunois also lived, belonged to Adam Oortmans, the husband of her aunt, Petronella de la Court, who around the same time put together the dolls' house now in the Central Museum in Utrecht.

Another nice object in the cellar is the syringe, here made of silver, which was used for cleaning windows. It was first filled with clean water from a bucket by pulling up the piston by its wooden knob. When this was pushed down hard, the water could be spouted metres high on to the windows.

a Storage jars with herbs

Glass and leather

Height 3.5 cm

b Barrels, tubs and wooden shoes

Maple

Height (barrel) 5.2 cm

a

b

The Kitchen

Petronella Dunois furnished her kitchen mainly with silver. Apart from such built-in features as the wall cupboards, the pump and the chimneypiece, only the chairs with their fat green cushions are mentioned in the inventory. There then follows a long list of kitchen equipment, all made of silver.

Among the innumerable silver toys made in the 17th century, household objects were often reproduced in miniature, probably also as playthings for the daughters of well-to-do parents. For her dolls' house Petronella could draw on an existing stock of pots, pans, dishes, gridirons, colanders, bowls, kettles, tongs and brooms, but this resulted in the proportions in the kitchen not always being very precise. It probably never occurred to her to have these objects made in miniature in brass or iron as Petronella Oortman was later to do for her dolls' house. Even the handles and taps of the pump, the spit with the two roast chickens, the plate rack and the tankard holder are of silver. Most of the objects bear the marks of the Amsterdam silversmiths Wessel Jansen and Michiel Maenbeeck.

Although no special mention is made of them anywhere, more of the objects must have belonged among the original contents of the kitchen. The chimney-piece pelmet, for instance, is made of the same green woollen cloth as the cushions. The wooden utensils and the speckled brown earthenware are also found in other 17th-century dolls' houses.

When this dolls' house was restored in 1982, the kitchen's original paper wall covering with a printed tile pattern was brought to light again.

a Spoon rack, by Wessel Jansen
Silver
Height 10 cm

b Roasting spit, by Michiel Maenbeeck
Silver
Height 3 cm

c Cooking pot, cake pan, coal pans, bottles and brazier
Earthenware
Height (bottle) 3 cm

a

b

c

The room next to the kitchen is called the 'Dining Room' in the old inventory. The table heavily laden with 17th-century silver dishes, plates and braziers certainly points in that direction, as do the various pans and kettles. The original inventory also included a salt cellar and a cruet for mustard, oil, vinegar and pepper, both made of silver. In the 18th century a large quantity of glassware was added, including glasses with enamel-twist stems and an extensive coffee service of painted white glass, which is displayed in the 17th-century glass-fronted cupboard.

A gentleman and his son would not normally have received a peasant in Waterland costume with his little boy in the dining room. The peasant lad, whose name is Teunis, has even brought his kite indoors. Perhaps he and his father had come to deliver foodstuffs. This dolls' house has no office or 'comptoir', where suppliers were normally dealt with, and that a business transaction is in progress here is evident from the original presence of an inkwell, a container for sand and a candle.

The walls of the dining room are lined with 'pictures' in wide black frames. They include two early 17th-century unsigned drawings on parchment behind glass, a little boy and a portrait of a gentleman, both in their original frames of dark whalebone, a beautiful shiny material which was used as a substitute for ebony in the second quarter of the 17th century. The picture over the cupboard, an Annunciation, is painted on alabaster. Those of saints have rather simpler frames. Such hand-coloured prints, often copies after great masters, were exported in great quantities in the 17th century from the Southern Netherlands. One of those here is signed by a minor engraver of Antwerp.

a **Portraits of a man and a boy, artist unknown, 2nd quarter of the 17th century**
Drawing on parchment, frames oak and whalebone
Height 12.1 and 11 cm
b **Head of Waterland peasant**
c **Son of the master of the house**
Height 16 cm

a

b

c

The American Association for Marriage and Family Therapy

promotes and advances the common professional

interests of Marriage and Family Therapists.

This document is published by:

The American Association for Marriage and Family Therapy

112 South Alfred Street

Alexandria, VA 22314-3061

703-838-9808